Revelation
WHEN ALL THINGS
BECOME NEW

Joseph M. Stowell

ZondervanPublishingHouse
Grand Rapids, Michigan

A Division of HarperCollins*Publishers*

CONTENTS

GREAT BOOKS OF THE BIBLE

Every book of the Bible is important, because each one is inspired by God. But certain books draw us to them time and again for their strong encouragement, powerful teaching, and practical wisdom. The Great Books of the Bible Series brings into one collection eight biblical books that distinguish themselves either because of their undisputed excellence or because they are perennial favorites.

The Psalms, with their poetic imagery, help us express our emotions to God and see the myriad ways God works during the best and worst times of our lives. Two books—Proverbs in the Old Testament and James in the New Testament—offer practical wisdom for dealing with the decisions and realities of everyday life. The gospel of John gives us the most intimate and personal view of Jesus, the God-become-man who is Savior and Lord.

Three books are letters written by the apostle Paul. Romans is Paul's masterpiece—the clearest and fullest explanation of the gospel found in Scripture; there we see our world through God's eyes. Philippians shows us how to experience joy when we are under pressure. Ephesians explores the crucial role of the church as a living community, giving us just a little taste of heaven on earth as we seek to serve the Lord.

The series ends where the Bible does—with Revelation, the last book of the Bible, where we glimpse our glorious future, when all things will become new.

Whether you are a new student of God's Word or one who has studied these books many times before, you will find here new insights and fresh perspectives that will make the Bible come alive for you.

The Great Books of the Bible Series is designed to be flexible. You can use the guides in any order. You can use them individually or in a small group or Sunday school class. Some of the guides have six studies; others have as many as thirteen. Moreover, these books help us discover what the Bible says rather than simply telling us the answers. The questions encourage us to think and explore options rather than merely filling in the blanks with one-word answers.

5

Leader's notes are provided in the back of each guide. They show how to lead a group discussion, provide additional information on questions, and suggest ways to deal with problems that may come up in the discussion. With such helps, someone with little or no experience can lead an effective study.

Suggestions for Individual Study

1. Begin each study with prayer. Ask God to help you understand the passage and to apply it to your life.

2. A good modern translation, such as the *New International Version,* the *New American Standard Bible,* or the *New Revised Standard Version,* will give you the most help. Questions in this guide are based on the *New International Version.*

3. Read and reread the passage(s). You must know what the passage says before you can understand what it means and how it applies to you.

4. Write your answers in the spaces provided in the study guide. This will help you to express clearly your understanding of the passage.

5. Keep a Bible dictionary handy. Use it to look up unfamiliar words, names, or places.

Suggestions for Group Study

1. Come to the study prepared. Careful preparation will greatly enrich your time in group discussion.

2. Be willing to join in the discussion. The leader of the group will not be lecturing, but will encourage people to discuss what they have learned in the passage. Plan to share what God has taught you in your individual study.

3. Stick to the passage being studied. Base your answers on the verses being discussed rather than on outside authorities such as commentaries or your favorite author or speaker.

4. Try to be sensitive to the other members of the group. Listen attentively when they speak, and be affirming whenever you can. This will encourage more hesitant members of the group to participate.

5. Be careful not to dominate the discussion. By all means participate! But allow others to have equal time.

6. If you are the discussion leader, you will find additional suggestions and helpful ideas in the leader's notes at the back of the guide.

WHEN ALL THINGS BECOME NEW

If you are like me, you have several unfinished projects lying around the house—including some that have been unfinished for a long time. Our basements, garages, and closets become repositories for the things we have lost interest in, have not had time for, or have lacked the resources to bring to completion.

The book of Revelation is about God's completion of some very significant unfinished business. When he created the universe—the material world, the animals, and mankind as the pinnacle of all he created—it was a perfect, stellarly beautiful display of his wisdom and power. And it was cumulatively a resounding statement to his magnificent glory. But then our adversary entered the scene, raped the landscape of man's relationship to his God, and left the universe, the world, and the human race damaged property. All were scarred by the effects of Satan's intrusion and were left hopelessly separated from God.

Since that point in history, God has been working to remedy the fall and reclaim all that he lost. Unlike many of us, he has neither lost interest nor lacked the resources to finish the task. In the sovereign scheme of things he has designed that all of history will ultimately culminate in the final defeat and abolition of Satan and the re-creation of a new heaven and a new earth. In the great New Jerusalem God will dwell with the redeemed of all time in an environment filled with eternal fulfillment, satisfaction, joy, and the celebration of his glory with no possibility that it will ever again be lost to the dominion of Satan and the hordes of hell.

The book of Revelation is about God's completion of the project of redemption. Although we have often regarded this book in terms of details about the last days, the primary feature of this book is not eschatological detail, but the person, work, and power of Christ. It is he who has been assigned the responsibility to effect the final doom of our adversary and the restoration of mankind and all of creation to God the Father. After this study is over, our view of the worth, value, power, mercy, and grace of Christ should be greatly expanded; it is my prayer that when that happens, we will find ourselves developing a deepening intimacy with him as our Lord and Savior and Friend.

Revelation not only points us to Christ as conqueror and consummator, but also reveals to us the deep and deadly grip that Satan has on our world and the people who populate this planet. Sin is never so obvious, and the stubbornness of fallen man never so forthright, as in the book of Revelation. This book demonstrates both the reality and the awesome strength of the powers of hell, and as such, it should give us a glimpse of our need for power beyond ourselves to confront the spiritual warfare that surrounds us.

A proper understanding of the book of Revelation, with all of its futuristic detail and symbolism, should strike into the heart of every believer a sense of confidence, courage, and assurance that at the end of all things God will reign in eternal victory and that we will enjoy the privilege of his presence forever.

The readings requested in the following studies encompass the entire text of the book of Revelation. Although in some instances a study will include several whole chapters, keep in mind that much of the book is colorful narrative that makes for fairly fast reading.

Needless to say, the symbols, metaphors, and references throughout the book of Revelation are challenging in terms of their interpretation to even the finest biblical scholar. The format of our study is meant simply to give you a beginning point for understanding this book and its relevance to your life. For further, in-depth study of the details of the book, let me recommend a few commentaries that can be helpful in your taking the next step: Alan Johnson, *The Expositor's Bible Commentary,* vol. 12 (Grand Rapids: Zondervan, 1981); Merrill C. Tenney, *Interpreting Revelation* (Grand Rapids: Eerdmans, 1957); John F. Walvoord, *The Revelation of Jesus Christ: A Commentary* (Chicago: Moody Press, 1966); Charles C. Ryrie, *Revelation,* Everyman's Bible Commentary (Chicago: Moody Press, 1968).

It is my prayer that this study will stimulate our minds and hearts toward a glad and spontaneous commitment to Christ and fill us with confident joy to face the troubles of life in the light of our secured future in Christ's finished work of redemption.

STUDY 1
THE INCOMPARABLE CHRIST

REVELATION 1:1-20

The last full eclipse of the sun that I experienced took place on a beautiful sun-drenched day with the backdrop of a cloudless, deep-blue sky. As the eclipse approached, an increasingly eerie sense of gray began to envelop the beauty of the day until finally Chicago was covered with semi-darkness. I have often wondered since then if that is not exactly what happens to our lives when lesser things eclipse the brilliance of Jesus Christ. The dullness and dimness of our perspective may very well be directly in proportion to how preeminent the incomparable Christ is to us.

As I watched the eclipse, I found it interesting that the sphere that was created to be reflective of the sun and lend the sun's light to the night misplaced itself and instead of being reflective became an impediment to the light. God has given us myriad things as instruments to reflect his grace and glory, but these somehow get misplaced and instead of reflecting him get in the way of him. Our treasures, our friends, our plans, and our dreams—all have a way of slowly becoming more important to us than Christ. Like the sun to our galaxy, Jesus Christ is the entity of incomparable worth and value to us. He is, as Paul proclaimed, the one who in all things must have the preeminence (Colossians 1:18).

11

1. What are some things in life that capture your attention or make your day or strike a sense of awe, anticipation, and wonder in your heart or preoccupy your heart or fill you with gratitude?

   Where does Christ place on your list, and why? If he is not on your list, why not?

2. Read Revelation 1:1–11. In what ways are our lives blessed when we read, hear, and do God's Word (v. 3)?

3. What enrichments do grace and peace bring to your life (v. 4)?

   In what ways do you receive them from each member of the Trinity?

4. In light of the incomparable credentials of Christ, what significance do the terms assigned to Christ in verse 5 have?

5. Contemplate the reality that this Christ has a personal relationship with you. List the ways in which his active love toward you—his act of liberating you, cleansing you, transferring you into his kingdom (Colossians 1:13), and giving you a privileged position as a priest to God—makes a difference in your life (vv. 5–6).

6. What would change in your life if you lived in the constant awareness that Christ was coming to take you home (v. 7)?

7. In what ways is Christ the Alpha and Omega in all of time and eternity (vv. 7–8)? In your life?

   Think of the most powerful and awe-inspiring persons of influence that you know or know of. How do they compare with this claim of Christ?

8. If you were to think of the community of believers around you as fellow Christians in terms of suffering, submission to Christ, and a non-negotiated faithfulness to Christ, what difference would it make in your actions and responses to one another (v. 9)?

9. How do you reconcile the mistaken notion that Revelation is an obscure, mystical, difficult-to-understand book with the fact that it was written to real, common folk in busy population centers where churches were struggling to maintain their purity and focus on Christ (v. 11)?

10. When you think of Christ, what thoughts and images come to your mind?

Read the description of Christ in verses 12–16 and visualize his strength, power, grandeur, and all-compelling presence. What is your response to this passage?

11. Given Christ's claims in verses 17–18, why do we have nothing to fear?

Memory Verse Look, he is coming with the clouds, and every eye will see him, even those who pierced him; and all the people of the earth will mourn because of him. So shall it be! Amen. "I am the Alpha and the Omega," says the Lord God, "who is, and who was, and who is to come, the Almighty."

—Revelation 1:7–8

Take time to list the specific ways in which Christ has worth and value to you. Use this list as a guide in your prayer time to focus your heart and gratitude to the Lord for the experienced reality of his presence in your life. As you make this prayer list a habit of your heart, meditate on the tendencies in your life to have lesser things eclipse his grandeur and glory, and envision how you would handle those occasions, persons, or experiences differently if Christ really were to be held by you as the incomparable treasure of your life.

Study 2
Great Expectations
Revelation 2:1 – 11

Most of our lives are continually victimized by the expectations of others: our spouses, our children, our bosses, our colleagues, our friends. Tethered to our activities and schedules, we find ourselves being yanked here and there, trying to please others and to live up to what they think we ought to do.

Throughout the New Testament Jesus Christ calls us to loosen the tethers with those around us and lasso our hearts to him. He calls us to know what he expects of us and to seek simply and only to please him. This singular focus and willing alignment with his expectations leads to a life that is not only pleasing to him but ultimately pleasing to others as well.

The letters to the seven churches are an effort on the part of Christ to express clearly what he expects and to draw his followers into alignment regardless of the cost.

1. If Christ were to write you a letter, what would he say to you in commendation?

What would he reveal as a concern?

2. Read Revelation 2:1–11. What difference would it make if you were constantly aware of the presence of Christ in your life (v. 1)?

3. Christ commends the church of Ephesus for their good works, hard work, steadfastness, distaste for evil, tenacity for doctrinal purity, and tireless endurance for his sake (vv. 2–3). Using these six accolades as a measure of what pleases Christ, reflect on your own life.

4. Since it is possible to become consumed with good behavior and yet displease God with less-than-pure motives, what questionable motives can underlie works that are good (v. 4)?

5. List the duties you perform for Christ. Put a check by those that are motivated by a grateful heart of love for Christ, and write out the reason that you do the others.

6. Recall a time when all you did for Christ was done because of your underlying love for him. Using your list, work through a process of repentance, recommitting yourself one item at a time to doing everything that you do for him and because of him.

7. What would your life be like if God removed his grace, enablement, and power (v. 5)? Be specific.

8. What would be different in your life if you lived here in light of your eternal reward (vv. 7, 11)?

9. Why should we expect a measure of suffering here on earth, especially in light of our commitment to Christ (v. 9)?

10. Compare your material wealth to the riches we have in Christ. As you list them, *honestly* think through what you value most—earthly or spiritual riches (v. 9).

11. What kind of attitude is fostered by the accumulation of earthly treasures (v. 9)?

    What kind of attitude develops in a life that places the highest value on riches in Christ?

12. When we think about impending suffering or find ourselves in the midst of it, what are some common fears that often paralyze us spiritually (v. 10)?

What truths in the verse serve to alleviate the fear factor?

13. One purpose in trouble is that we are tested regarding the reality of our faith in Christ (v. 10; James 1:3). What aspects of our Christianity are put on display when trouble comes?

Memory Verse "He who has an ear, let him hear what the Spirit says to the churches. To him who overcomes, I will grant to eat from the tree of life, which is in the paradise of God."

—Revelation 2:7

Between Studies

Two of the key expectations that God has for us relate to the purity of our motives and a willingness to graciously suffer for him if need be. Measure the ways in which your life squares with these important desires of God for us.

Discuss with your spouse or a trusted friend the motives that you struggle with, and list the ways in which you would be willing to suffer for him if he calls you to do so.

Study 3
First Things First
Revelation 2:12 – 3:6

Think of how much time we spend standing in line—from grocery stores to ticket windows to bus stops to the cafeteria, at banks, airports, restrooms, and crowded public events. Even if we try to beat the system by getting there early enough to be first in line, we will still have to wait for the doors to open.

In some lines we take numbers, as in the wonderful bakery where my wife, Martie, and I like to buy doughnuts early in the morning. Amid the crowd of persons and things that move around our lives, we have the capacity to assign numbers to those that will be first. In the midst of all of this, Christ keeps asking our hearts where he stands in the line of our living. He seeks to be first—and deserves to be first. He has every right to hold the unchallenged priority in our lives, not only in our respect and worship, but also in our submission to his authority and faithfulness to his Word.

What number have you assigned to Christ? Who or what is in front of him? Would we really want to say to a watching world that those entities are more important than he is?

1. Although our society has all but eliminated God from its fabric, it remains incurably religious. What are our culture's gods, and what kind of morality or lack of morality results from the worship of these gods?

What are the false notions that undergird this cultural worship and behavior?

2. Read Revelation 2:12–17. What are the idols that are the most compelling in your world (v. 13)?

3. Reflect on the history of Scripture and our present society. How has Satan used immorality in his attempts to destroy God's plan (v. 13)?

4. In what ways do you remain faithful to Christ in the face of the seduction of idolatrous and immoral pressures?

5. What external pressures are you forced to resist to keep Christ completely on the throne?

6. Even in not being idolatrous, can you identify areas of compromise that Christ would find offensive in your life? As you identify these, work through a time of genuine repentance and build points of accountability to enable you to maintain purity before him.

7. If removing an idol or a specific matter of compromise creates a sense of need or loss, what provision of Christ is sufficient to supply for you what you thought your sin and idolatrous substitute would supply (v. 17)?

8. Read Revelation 2:18–29. Trace a history of your Christian experience. Consider whether you have a life characterized by more good deeds now (such as forgiveness, generosity, purity, compassion for the poor and the lost, patience with irritants in life), or whether your good works are on the decline since you first met Christ (vv. 18–19). Be specific.

9. Since not everything within the context of Christianity (such as church, television, seminars, books, tapes) is within the scope of God's revealed truth, what standards of purity and authenticity would you apply (vv. 20–23)?

What factors make false teaching in the context of the church alluring?

10. What acts of undaunted faithfulness in this life will have an effect on our lives in the world to come (vv. 26–28)?

11. Read Revelation 3:1–6. In what ways might we as Christians have a name that is alive, yet have lives that are dead (v. 1)?

12. List the aspects of your life in Christ that you have grown satisfied with and yet know that there is still room to grow into a greater sense of his likeness (v. 2).

13. What are the areas of our lives that need to be purified to enable us to be worthy of his fellowship both here and in eternity (vv. 4–5)?

Memory Verse "He who overcomes will, like them, be dressed in white. I will never blot out his name from the book of life, but will acknowledge his name before my Father and his angels."

—Revelation 3:5

Between Studies

Throughout Scripture, idolatry has not just been viewed dimly by God but has also been a justifiable reason for his judgment. Think of all that you have and everyone whom you know. Reflect on your house, your garage, the workplace, your family, and your social circles. Think of your dreams and plans for the rest of your life. Which of these entities has the potential to supplant God as the rightful ruler in your life, as the one to be valued and treasured above anything else?

Envision a space between you and Christ that is cluttered with these entities that keep getting in the way. Start moving toward Christ, and envision yourself setting these things to the side, so that nothing stands between as you take steps toward him in an effort to clear the way.

STUDY 4
OPPORTUNITY KNOCKS
REVELATION 3:7 – 22

Coming to know Christ as personal Savior and Lord and then growing in our knowledge and understanding of him opens us to new
vistas and wider horizons than we have ever known before. As in so
many occasions in life, these opportunities are here for the taking,
but once denied may be unavailable in their fullest and richest mea-
sures in the days and the years to come. And while it is not true that
with Christ opportunity knocks but once, it is true that opportunities
neglected diminish our usefulness in service of his kingdom.

As we shall note in this study, Christ provides a broad range of
opportunities that make a significant difference in how we live. Opportunities for fellowship, empowerment, identification, and reliance on
his sufficiency are among the privileges he offers us.

1. List at least five opportunities that are uniquely yours in
   Jesus Christ. Evaluate in what measure you have seized
   these opportunities for his glory.

2. Read Revelation 3:7–13. What difference does it make (v. 7)
   that Christ

   — Is holy?

25

— Is true?

— Holds the keys of David?

— Opens and shuts doors of opportunity?

3. When we feel overwhelmed by our own inadequacies, what empowerment from Christ strengthens and emboldens us (v. 8)?

4. Reflect on the normal cycle of a day's activities. What are your greatest challenges to keeping God's Word and not denying his name?

5. When you consider the long view of life and eternity, what will be the final results in the lives of those who oppose your stand for Christ (v. 9)? (See also Philippians 2:9–11.)

   What does this truth engender in your heart in the face of personal or societal opposition and intimidation?

6. If you believed that Christ would not permit you to be over-whelmed by the outpouring of his wrath and that he was coming quickly to take you to all that is "far better," in what ways would your courage and perseverance be enhanced (vv. 10–11)?

7. Given that we proudly wear designer labels on our clothes, identifying ourselves with trendy and upscale names, think of the privilege of wearing his name and the name of his city (v. 12). In what ways can we wear his name now for others to see our identity with him (T-shirts and bumper stickers excluded)?

8. Read Revelation 3:14–22. Think of the grandeur of all that is in the universe. What does it tell you about Christ, who is the creator, sustainer, and supreme entity of all that is around us (v. 14)? (See also Colossians 1:13–18.)

9. In what ways do we deceive ourselves into thinking that we are pleasing to God, when in reality our lives may be nauseating to him (vv. 15–17)?

10. Riches often blind us to our true needs. They provide a false sense of well-being, comfort, and self-sufficiency. How can we as believers develop a sense of our sufficiency in Christ, see ourselves as God sees us, and be willing to suffer loss when necessary to maintain undefiled purity?

11. What are the sources of God's loving discipline in our lives? How do we respond (vv. 19–20)?

12. What steps would you take to tear down the barriers to unhindered fellowship with Christ and to cultivate a growing intimacy with him (v. 20)?

Memory Verse "Here I am! I stand at the door and knock. If anyone hears my voice and opens the door, I will come in and eat with him, and he with me."

—Revelation 3:20

Between Studies

Read Revelation 3 again and list the opportunities that you would like to undertake on behalf of Christ. Pray through this list of new adventures and plan specifically how you might follow through.

By contrast, recall opportunities you may have seized in the past that, while promising good and appealing results, led you into spiritual poverty and were distasteful to God.

The Worthy-to-Be-Worshiped Christ

Revelation 4 – 5

H istory is full of pictures of thousands upon thousands of persons gathered in public squares or along motorcade routes to celebrate, cheer, and proclaim the praises of earthly rulers. Yet these come and go, and others stand in their place to receive the same cheers of the massive crowds.

But above all of the earth's monarchs there is One who is eternally worthy of all of our heartfelt praise and affirmation, not only because of what he has done and will do for us, but simply because of who he is.

The word *worship* is a form of the word *worth* with *ship* tagged on the end, not unlike calling a ruler "his lordship"—that is, one who is lord. The concept of worship literally means our attitude toward one who is "worthy of our celebrant acclamation of praise."

Through this study we will seek to gain a sense of the worthiness of Christ that enables us spontaneously and willingly to ascribe to him the worship that is due his name.

1. Read Revelation 4. Putting yourself in John's place—in the presence of the God of heaven—what would be your own response and the impact on your life after you had returned to earth (v. 1)?

2. Since we may often feel that evil is triumphant, unrestrained, and unchecked, what does it mean for us that the conquest and resolution of evil "must take place after this"? (See also Psalm 73 and 1 Corinthians 15:20–28.)

3. Why do you think God's sitting on the throne is described in such colorful imagery (vv. 2–3)?

What are your feelings as you read about God's throne in heaven?

Likewise, the elders' thrones, their robes of white, and the golden crowns on their heads (v. 4)?

4. In what ways do the four creatures represent qualities of God that are worthy to be praised (vv. 5–7)?

5. If you could see and therefore know everything as the eye-filled four creatures do, in what specific ways would your worship be affected (v. 8)?

30

6. Think of the creatures celebrating the grand worth of the everlasting, holy, and all-powerful God, and then envision yourself falling before him with the elders. What symbols of position, power, authority, or pride could you cast at his feet in submissive allegiance to him as the rightful ruler of your life (vv. 8–11)?

7. Read Revelation 5. Describe what your life might be like if there were no final redemption, no ultimate defeat of Satan, no just conclusion to existence. Then rejoice to realize that Christ, through the cross and his resurrection, is the only one worthy and qualified to break the seals and unfold the plan of redemption to completion (vv. 1–7).

8. In what ways is prayer a difficult spiritual discipline for you?

   How would your prayer life be different if you always kept in mind that your prayers are used in heaven as a fragrant incense in worship to the Lamb of God (v. 8)? (See also Revelation 8:3–4.)

9. In what ways are we, according to verse 10,
   — A kingdom?

   — Priests to our God?

How can we express these privileges in a concrete way in our daily experience?

10. How can we practically give honor, glory, and dominion to Christ through our lives as a regular act of worship and praise?

Memory Verse "You are worthy, our Lord and God, to receive glory and honor and power, for you created all things, and by your will they were created and have their being."

—Revelation 4:11

Between Studies

Think about a person to whom you readily give honor. Whom do you adore? Whom do you so admire and respect that you are quick to affirm them, not only to his or her face, but to others as well?

Meditate on ways to live with an ongoing spirit of praise, adoration, and worship toward Christ. How would your life be different if you lived in that perspective?

STUDY 6
THE LAMB:
THE MERCIFUL JUDGE

REVELATION 6:1 – 8:5

one of us likes to face judgment, nor do we normally like to think of others being judged. Thoughts of a God who is all love and peace form a picture of God that is widely prevalent today, but a picture that is inaccurate and incomplete. God is not only love and peace; he is also justice.

If they thought further about it, the people who see only a kind and loving God might indeed decide they want a God who is also just. We certainly would not want our courts to be ruled by judges who did not have a sense of justice. In a world without a reinforced system of justice, treacherous people would roam the streets, able to carry out their violent schemes with no fear of repudiation or sense of remorse. And because not all evildoers—whether common criminals or wicked rulers—are called to account in this life, we want a God who will ultimately and finally judge all that is and has been wrong in our world.

Yet the beautiful thing about God is that he is a balanced, beneficial combination of all his qualities. And in that, he is like no other being. Although he is a just God and will judge sin, he is also a merciful, loving, and gracious God who sent his Son, the Lamb, to provide forgiveness in the place of condemnation and heaven in the place of hell. If his mercy eclipses his justice then he is no longer God. And if his justice is without mercy, then he denies himself. The Cross stands as a monument in history where justice and mercy are perfectly combined in the death of the Lamb of God, Jesus Christ our Savior and Lord.

1. When you think of God's judgment, what are your feelings, and how do you think people in general feel about it? Do you recoil from the thought, or do you see positive significance in divine justice?

   What would be the consequences of a world without a God who did not ultimately deal with all that is wrong?

2. Read again Revelation 5:1–5. The seals need to be broken in order to unfold the culmination of redemptive history. What do these verses suggest as to the strength of Satan's grip on the earth?

3. Read Revelation 6:1–17. Describe in your own words the effect on the earth and its population as Christ breaks each successive seal.

4. What in your life is worth dying for (v. 9)?

   What will give us the strength and courage to die for Christ if we are called to do so?

5. With the sixth seal, people recognize the judgment of God, yet their response is to hide instead of coming to him in repentance pleading for mercy (vv. 12–17). Suggest some reasons why people would respond this way. What does this say about the heart of mankind?

In what ways are you stubborn about sin in your life?

6. Read Revelation 7:1–17. When we go through crises and trials, what assurance do we have that God will hold back anything that would harm us until he has secured our ultimate safety and provided his seal of security (vv. 1–3)?

7. The reality and availability of God's mercy is interjected between the sixth and seventh seals of God's judgment, as 144,000 Jews and a countless multitude of Gentiles come to salvation during this time of intense divine intervention in human history. In what specific ways have you been a recipient of God's mercy, and what has been your response to him as a result (vv. 4–17)?

8. When you think of Christ as shepherd, what concepts come to your mind (v. 17)?

What specific benefits come to us as a result of Christ's dual ministry as comforting shepherd and righteous judge?

9. Read Revelation 8:1–5. Note the prevalence of the work of angels throughout the book of Revelation, both in the churches (chs. 2–3) and in the unfolding of the last things (chs. 6–19). To understand the role of angels in the world today, begin to make a list of their activities and attitudes as reflected in Revelation.

What has Revelation taught us to this point in regard to angels, their activities, and their attitudes?

10. How do you think the angels viewed these judgments, considering that they were present when their fellow angel, Lucifer, led a rebellion against God?

11. Why do we tend to resist the reality of God's judgment?

How is our perspective on judgment affected by our understanding of sin?

Memory Verse "Never again will they hunger; never again will they thirst. The sun will not beat upon them, nor any scorching heat. For the Lamb at the center of the throne will be their shepherd; he will lead them to springs of living water. And God will wipe away every tear from their eyes."

—Revelation 7:16–17

Between Studies

Think of how your life—your motives, activities, attitudes, relationships, and responses—would be an appropriate target of the justice of God. Think of standing before him and suddenly feeling the weight of the guilt of all that you have done in your life to deserve his judgment. Then think about the Lamb that was slain on Calvary for you. Envision the weight of that just, responsive God, transitioning your judgment onto the shoulders of Christ. Sense one more time the cleansing work of his merciful redemption, and remind yourself of how you felt when you finally came to him and he lifted the weight and washed you all the way to the core.

TROUBLE AND TRIUMPH

REVELATION 8:5 – 11:19

It was a dark day in my boyhood experience when my dad would say to me on Saturday morning, "Before you go and play with your friends, I want you to weed the garden." The agony was not just the delayed gratification of neighborhood baseball, but the horrible prospect of having to go through the trouble of doing the task that I disliked the most. Worse than homework, clam chowder, liver, and wearing a tie was the thought of weeding the garden. Yet, when the task was done, there came a certain sense of satisfaction in seeing the beauty of the garden that now had been rid of all that had distracted and defaced its intended glory.

Trouble often precedes triumph in life, in far more strategic and serious ways than simply weeding a garden. It has taken great wars to rid our planet of tyrannical despots. It takes deep and delicate surgery to restore health and life, labor pains to give birth to a child, and sometimes suffering to preserve a nonnegotiable value.

And so it is in the end times, when God will have to pour out his wrath upon the enemies of all that is holy and just and true in order that his righteous and wonderful reign might finally be established.

As we work through these chapters full of drama and ultimate victory, the principle that God-ordained trouble can bring great triumph and benefits needs to undergird not only our sense of the future culmination of redemption, but our everyday struggles as well.

1. In light of the increasing evil and decadence all around us, what biblical assurances do we have that keep us dedicated to God and free from a sense of despair and defeat in our spirit?

2. Read Revelation 8:6–13. List the targets of the first four trumpet judgments and identify how mankind has used and abused these aspects of his creation in ways not intended by God.

   In what ways do people worship the creation rather than the Creator?

3. Mankind tends to view creation as a source of supply and nourishment without recognizing God as the provider and creator. Why do you suppose the godless persist in their sense of self-sufficiency even in the face of diminishing resources of the created world?

4. In what ways might our human-centered focus on environmentalism be offensive to God?

5. Read Revelation 9:1–20. Of what significance is it that the angel of God had control over the demons in hell (vv. 13–16; see also Revelation 7:1–3)?

6. What do we learn from this passage about demons and their dealings with mankind (vv. 4–11)?

   How would this relate to the ultimate purpose behind Satan's seductions in our lives and the increasing prevalence of the occult in America?

7. Much of the work of angels is focused toward the restriction of evil, as in verses 13–14. How would our attitudes or behavior change if we were mindful of the supernatural, unseen restraint of evil that is exercised on our behalf?

8. Why do you think mankind would stubbornly refuse to repent even after such humbling judgment by God (vv. 20–21)?

   What does this tell you about the nature of our hearts?

9. Note the list of sins that characterizes the earth in verses 20–21. How do they relate to the preceding judgments?

How do they relate to prevalent patterns of living in our own culture? In our own lives?

10. Read Revelation 10:1–11. In what way does God's Word "taste sweet," create pain within, and empower us to speak authoritatively about sin and righteousness in any land or culture (vv. 8–11)?

11. Read Revelation 11:1–10. Given the miraculous signs that the witnesses used to authenticate their ministry, why do you suppose they were rejected?

Why did the whole world celebrate their death?

12. Read Revelation 11:11–14. What do the resurrection and ascension of the witnesses tell you about God's power over Satan and God's ability to bring glory out of Satan's finest moments of opposition?

How can you appropriate God's power in your life in the face of Satan's attacks?

13. Read Revelation 11:15–19. Ultimately, God will judge what is wrong and securely reign in righteousness forever. In what ways does this truth stengthen your loyalty to God regardless of opposition (see also Revelation 10:7)?

Memory Verse "The kingdom of the world has become the kingdom of our Lord and of his Christ, and he will reign for ever and ever. . . . We give thanks to you, Lord God Almighty, the One who is and who was, because you have taken your great power and have begun to reign."

—Revelation 11:15, 17

Between Studies

Reflect on times in your life when God used trouble as a prelude to triumph. Think of specific results and beneficial lessons learned.

What troubles are you facing now? As you meditate on the principles offered in this study, have faith that God will bring triumph for his glory, prove his power over Satan, create a testimony to his authority to rule and reign.

The Night Before Christmas

Revelation 12

O n that first night before Christmas, there was something more than houses where creatures weren't stirring and children were sleeping with visions of sugarplums dancing in their sweet little heads. There was a dark, invisible positioning of the powers of hell against the birth of this One who would bring ultimate defeat to the domain of Satan. These forces of the night against the Messiah broke out through the edict of Herod, who commanded that all the male children two and under should be killed. These forces advanced their cause through the political and religious powers of Christ's day. Then their struggle for supremacy reached its pinnacle when they victoriously nailed the Messiah to an instrument of ancient torture.

But their apparent victory was short-lived. Three days later, the *Son* rose, and the dawn of redemption was assured. As he ascended to heaven, the victory was secured and the bitter anger of the defeated foe expressed itself in rage toward the nation that had been selected to birth the Conqueror.

When we think of Christmas and the birth of Christ, we must think not so much of toys and tots, but of the reality that there is a spiritual warfare raging and that the true spirit of Christmas is the spirit of hard-won victory over sin. This spirit lives in the Messiah— and in our daily lives. We must remember that Satan focuses his wrath not only toward those who brought about the Messiah, but also toward those who carry the Messiah's message of victory today.

1. When you think of Satan, what specifically do you envision?

2. Read Revelation 12. How does this chapter change your perspectives on Satan?

   How is your awareness of the intensity of spiritual warfare heightened?

3. The mission of Israel was to bear the Messiah's seed to fruition (see Genesis 12:1–3). In light of the messianic promise, the Jewish people became, throughout history, a primary object of Satan's attack, both before the birth of Christ and afterward. The pain ("travail," KJV) mentioned in verse 2 is a reference to Israel's many troubles as the nation through whom the victor would come (vv. 1–2, 13, 17). Cite examples of her travail and consider the invisible work of Satan behind the curtain of history.

   In what ways does this place anti-Semitism in a new light for you?

4. What events surrounding the birth of Christ can be seen as Satan's attempt to "devour her child" (vv. 3–4)?

How about during Christ's life?

5. What did God do to miraculously preserve the mission and ministry of the Messiah?

   What does that tell you about the capacity of God to watch over us and grant us ultimate safety both on earth and finally in heaven (v. 5)?

6. Note again in verse 5 that Christ will be the ultimate and final ruler of all the kingdoms of the earth, fulfilling God's promises in Scripture . How does this help you trust God to faithfully keep all his promises regardless of the odds or resistance?

   Which of God's promises seem impossible to you?

7. God has always created places of refuge for his people, as indicated in verses 6 and 14. What places of refuge, both physical and spiritual, has God supplied for you in the midst of trouble?

8. Read again verses 7–9. In what specific ways do we share in Christ's victory over Satan

   — In our personal, daily walk?

   — In the ministry of Christ through us to others?

   — In the midst of suffering?

   — In spiritual disciplines

   — In death?

9. In what way does the ministry of Christ as our high priest and his work as advocate on our behalf relate to Satan's work of accusing us before God (see Hebrews 4:14–16)?

   How might Satan even now be accusing you before the Father's throne?

10. Satan was defeated at the Cross and now is finally cast out of heaven to the earth, yet he still has tremendous anger toward the human instruments of God's fatal blow to him and his purposes (vv. 13–17). What does that tell you about his attitude toward us as servants of God and proclaimers of the gospel?

Memory Verse

"Now have come the salvation and the power and the kingdom of our God, and the authority of his Christ. For the accuser of our brothers, who accuses them before our God day and night, has been hurled down. They overcame him by the blood of the Lamb and by the word of their testimony."

—Revelation 12:10–11

Between Studies

Consider specific ways by which Satan may have seduced you in the past through things that looked beneficial, pleasurable, and comfortable. Think about what may have been his destructive intentions.

Use these recollections as an impetus to a new sense of faithfulness and loyalty to the Christ who is already victorious.

STUDY 9

MARKED FOR GOOD

REVELATION 13 – 14

Some people in developing countries have initiation rites that include scarring their faces so as to identify themselves as members of a particular village or tribe. In a city like Chicago, people have other ways to tout their identity: wearing clothes that reflect an ethnic background, or wearing the bills of their caps as the trademark of a certain gang, or wearing a uniform that connotes a type of job. We all tend to bear certain marks of socioeconomic standing, cultural background, and even the region of the country where we live.

During the Great Tribulation there will only be two marks that really make a difference. Those who have the mark of the beast will be clearly and visibly identified with him and his cause; by contrast, a smaller group will carry the mark of their Father in heaven and, without intimidation, worship and praise his name. Actually, there are only two identities that people carry today: those who are identified with the fallen world system in terms of lifestyle, attitude, and activity, and those who are identified with the values and ethics of the kingdom of Christ. Tragically, sometimes it is hard from the outside to distinguish the latter from the former.

1. In what ways is your life clearly marked as a follower of the Lamb?

What aspects of your life sometimes bear an identity with the forces of our adversary?

2. Read Revelation 13:1–10. What aspects of the beast compelled mankind to follow and worship both him and Satan, who empowered him (vv. 1–4)?

   What do these verses tell you of Satan's ability to gain massive followings, and how do you see him accomplishing this in our culture today?

3. "Proud words and blasphemies" against God characterize the rule of Satan during his worldwide dominion in the second half of the tribulation. What precursors of that pattern of Satan can you see in the culture and society in which we live today (vv. 5–7)?

4. How is the life of a follower of Christ unique in contrast to the idolatrous worship of those who follow Satan (v. 8)?

5. What difference does it make in our lives that God will ultimately deal with those who persecute us (v. 10)? (See also Revelation 14:11–13.)

How does this truth affect your attitude toward people who make life difficult for you?

6. Read Revelation 13:11–18. As the second beast (also called the false prophet in Revelation 16:13) calls the earth to worship the antichrist, what specific tactic does he use to gain their allegiance (vv. 13–14)?

   What strategy does he use to force the world to worship the first beast (vv. 15–17)?

   In what ways do these patterns parallel Satan's work in the world today?

7. Read Revelation 14:1–5. Meditate on the glorious scene described: the Lamb on Mount Zion, surrounded by 144,000 faithful followers who sing praise to him with integrity and pure hearts. Consider how your life can become more clearly identified with Christ in the eyes of the people around you day by day.

8. How does being a follower of the Lamb affect your attitude, activity, relationships, priorities, and nourishment (vv. 4–5)?

9. Read Revelation 14:6–20. What is the significance for you of

— God's merciful invitation to all mankind for redemption (vv. 6–7)?

— The assurance of the judgment of even the most powerful systems of evil and its adherents (vv. 8–11, 14–20)?

— The security of the saints even in the face of death (vv. 12–13)?

Memory Verse "Fear God and give him glory, because the hour of his judgment has come. Worship him who made the heavens, the earth, the sea and the springs of water."

—Revelation 14:7

Between Studies

Think through the life of Christ (and if you want to take the time, review the Gospels). List the aspects of his life and ministry that clearly identified him with his Father but were in contrast to the religious, cultural, and political systems of his day. Use the list as a measurement for your own life; try to pinpoint the tactics of Satan that make you vulnerable to "switching identities." Consider how you will deal with these tactics from now on.

Study 10
I Don't Get Mad . . .

Revelation 15 – 16

We have all heard the retort, "I don't get mad; I just get even." After reading through the three series of judgments in the book of Revelation (the seals, the trumpets, and now the bowls), one might assume that God had finally gotten both mad at Satan, sin, and sinners and even with them for their phenomenal offenses throughout the history of mankind, dating back to Adam and Eve.

The truth is that in these judgments God is neither mad nor getting even. These judgments are a necessary response of a holy and just God to the destructive nature and effects of sin. If he had not finally carried out justice, he would have had to deny himself, and all of mankind could say that he was not a holy and just God. What should surprise us is not the massive scale of God's judgments, but that he waited so long.

Desiring that no one should perish but that all should come to repentance, God mercifully held off his judgment and gave maximum opportunity for mankind to come repentantly and receive his grace and forgiveness. But the depth of human hatred toward God has shown that the judgments only created deeper alienation and blasphemy.

We see throughout the book of Revelation that those who know God best and have opened their hearts to him do not judge him for his judgments; rather, they praise, worship, and affirm his actions as a normal and rightful extension of who he is. They feel a deep sense of gratitude for his redemptive work that carries them safely beyond judgment to his grace, mercy, and eternity.

55

1. What is your response to insult, injury, or injustice, and what are your feelings toward those who inflict them on you?

2. Read Revelation 15:1–4. In what specific ways is your response different from God's?

3. List the characteristics of God that are expressed in his judgments (vv. 3–4). In what way do these traits make judgment necessary?

   How do the characteristics affect your mental, emotional, and spiritual attitude toward a God of wrath and judgment?

4. What does it mean to "fear" God and "bring glory" to his name (v. 4)?

   What do you "fear," and what are you prone to want to glorify in your life?

5. Read Revelation 15:5–8. How does the temple symbolize that God's judgments are grounded in his holiness?

6. Read Revelation 16:1–7. Suppose "the mark of the beast" (v. 2) represents compromise and accommodation to culture. Discuss these verses in that light.

7. What gives us confidence and courage even in the face of our greatest enemies?

8. Read Revelation 16:8–21. Note the refusal to repent (vv. 9, 11). When God brings trouble to lead people to repentance, what are common human responses?

   How do you respond when trouble comes into your life?

9. What else might God accomplish in judgment besides demonstrating his holiness and justice (see verse 12)?

   What additional purposes might God have in mind when he seeks to purify us through his loving discipline?

10. Verse 15 tells us that Jesus can return unexpectedly at any moment. How would your life be different if that thought never left your mind? How would your actions and attitudes change?

11. Verses 17–21 signal the completion of the judgments of God on Satan, sin, and unrepentant sinners. Reflect on the themes that dominate Revelation 15–16 and their significance for us:

    — The depth of offense that sin is to a holy God

    — The breadth and depth of God's judgment on sin

    — The faithfulness of those who faced demonic pressure and intimidation

---

Memory Verse "Great and marvelous are your deeds, Lord God Almighty. Just and true are your ways, King of the ages. Who will not fear you, O Lord, and bring glory to your name? For you alone are holy. All nations will come and worship before you, for your righteous acts have been revealed."

—Revelation 15:3–4

Between Studies

Read Colossians 1 several times, focusing particularly on verses 9–29. Meditate on the person of Christ, his finished work on your behalf, and the privileged position he has given you as one of his own.

As a companion text, read and contemplate Romans 5:1–11 and 8:18–39.

Study 11
Clearing the Way

An amazing feat of modern engineering is the imploding of large, old buildings when it is necessary to clear a piece of city property to make way for a new, more glorious, more functional building. Tons of dynamite are strategically placed throughout the old building to pulverize it and cause it literally to fall in on itself without damaging adjacent buildings. When the dynamite is ignited, it leaves a self-contained pile of rubble for the bulldozers to take away.

This section of the book of Revelation tells of the coming day when God will implode the systems of this fallen world to clear the way for the systems of righteousness that will govern the New Jerusalem and the new heavens and the new earth.

Throughout history, Satan has used religion, political structures, and commercial gain to promote evil. The record is littered with corrupt power systems and tyrants. In the tribulation season that comes at the end of the history of this world, a one-world religious system will rise against God in support of the antichrist, only to have the beast himself and kings of this world rise up and devour her in a kind of self-implosion of that system. At that point the beast will elevate himself to supreme political power, calling on mankind to focus its religious instincts on him and worship him as god. At the end of the tribulation God will finally destroy this system—called "Babylon"—to clear the landscape in preparation for his great and glorious eternity.

    1.   Do you think of evil influence and activities as random offenses against God, or do you see instead a designed struc-

ture of the spiritual underworld capitalizing on the fallenness of creation? Explain.

How does your view affect your attitudes and outlook on
life?

2. Read Revelation 17:1–8. How have both non-Christian and
   pseudo-Christian religions

   — Been used as a tool of Satan?

   — Struck false and "immoral" relationships with
      governments (v. 2)?

   — Put adherents under a manipulative spell (v. 2)?

   — Blasphemed and betrayed the name of Christ (v. 3)?

   — Shed the blood of the faithful (v. 6)?

3. How can the church maintain its doctrinal purity in the face
   of false religions advanced in the cause of Satan?

4. What are some forms that false teaching might take today?
   (It may be helpful to recall the biblical accounts of Jesus'
   dealings with the religious leaders in his time.)

5. Read Revelation 17:9–18. Note that in time the beast, the antichrist, will no longer use religion to accomplish its ends, but will turn to political power to become an object of worship. What does this teach us about Satan's loyalty to those whom he uses to advance his purposes?

Recall a personal or public example when loyalty was betrayed and faithfulness disdained to advance one's self-interests.

6. In what ways is God willing to advance his cause by using Satan's finest moments in our lives?

What does this reveal about God's sovereignty over our lives (v. 17)?

7. Read chapter 18. What things are described as the objects of people's search for security?

Which of these are particular temptations for you?

What difference does it make when we view these things as the tools of Satan?

8. Who is said to rejoice, and why (v. 20)?

How did God judge Babylon on their behalf?

How does this account encourage us today?

Memory Verse "They will make war against the Lamb, but the Lamb will overcome them because he is Lord of lords and King of kings—and with him will be his called, chosen and faithful followers."

—Revelation 17:14

Between Studies

Reflect on the different ways evil is advancing in the world. Envision what it would be like for all these to be gathered into a one-world religious or political system.

Consider some new and specific ways that you can resist evil and remain faithful to Christ in daily life as the presence of evil surrounds you?

HOW SWEET IT WILL BE...

REVELATION 19 – 22

We have all tasted the sweet experience of a strategic victory at some point in our lives. Etched in my mind is the moment in the 1980 Winter Olympics in Lake Placid, New York, when the U.S. Hockey Team (which comprised amateurs instead of the veteran professionals of other teams) won the gold medal against great odds. This triumph came at a time when the United States was struggling through the Iranian hostage crisis and a failing, inflationary economy. That moment rallied the nation to a new sense of significance and confidence.

There is a sense in which the final victory of Christ over sin, death, and hell is like that come-from-behind Olympic vitory—although their scope, magnitude, depth, and eternal significance are without comparison.

These closing chapters of Revelation are a thrilling story of the unfolding conclusion of God's work to finish the business of redemption. They take us through Christ's millennial reign, when he will keep his promise to Israel to rule the earthly kingdom of David; to the great judgment throne, when all those who are his will be given final credentials to eternal glory, and the rest, along with Satan, will be cast into the lake of fire; to the entrance of his people into the New Jerusalem, the new heavens, and the new earth, where they will enjoy him forever.

All this will resound to the eternal glory of God, who not only promised victory but also gains it through his Son, Jesus Christ.

1. Make a list of the troubles, struggles, frustrations, and disappointments in your life. What practical difference does it make for you today to know that heaven is real, that victory is inevitable in Christ, and that all injustice will be reckoned with in the end?

2. What have you expected out of life in this present world?

   In what ways have you lived as if this is "the best of all possible worlds"?

3. Read Revelation 19:1–10. Envision the scene in heaven when the judgments are complete and the angelic host and elders stand on the verge of victory over the fallenness of the world (vv. 1–5). Think especially how the angels feel who have played a key role in the spiritual warfare against sin and Satan.

   How can you refocus your attention in order to live in anticipation of this ultimate moment of victory?

4. What pictures does the wedding dinner (vv. 7–8) bring to mind?

5. Why are we sometimes tempted to worship the messenger rather than the One who sent the messenger (v. 10)?

6. Read Revelation 19:11–21. Given all the ways we perceive of Christ—Friend, Savior, Lord, Redeemer, and so on—what difference does it make to envision him as a warrior (vv. 11–16)?

7. Why is it significant that Christ's robe is dipped in blood and that his name is the Word of God (v. 13)?

8. Read Revelation 20:1–10. How should the prospect of Christ's thousand-year reign and his ultimate defeat of Satan affect our daily lives?

9. What do we learn from Satan's persistence in hatred and opposition toward God at the end of the Millennium?

What do we learn from Satan's ability to deceive citizens of the millennial kingdom and induce them to rebellion (vv. 8–9)?

10. What would life be like in a world without Satan's influence and activity? Be specific.

11. Read Revelation 20:11–15. Picture yourself hearing your name read at the great throne of judgment and being granted safe passage into eternity. How would you express your gratitude and loyalty to Christ?

12. Read Revelation 21:1–22:6. What privileges does heaven hold for you? Compile a list and meditate on these privileges and rewards.

In what ways do the realities of heaven change your perspective on life here?

13. Read Revelation 22:7–21. What would it mean to live as if we expect Jesus to come tonight (vv. 7, 12–13)?

Memory Verse "Behold, I am coming soon! My reward is with me, and I will give to everyone according to what he has done. I am the Alpha and the Omega, the First and the Last, the Beginning and the End. Blessed are those who wash their robes, that they may have the right to the tree of life and may enter through the gates into the city."

—Revelation 22:12–14

Reflect on these three quotations:

"The only ultimate tragedy we can experience on earth is to feel at home here." —Malcolm Muggeridge

"Just think of stepping on shore and finding it heaven; of touching a hand and finding it God's; of breathing new air and finding it celestial; of waking up in glory and finding it home." —Don Wyrtzen

"But until then my heart will go on singing, / Until then with joy I'll carry on—/ Until the day my eyes behold the city, / Until the day God calls me home. —Stuart Hamblen

LEADER'S NOTES

eading a Bible discussion—especially for the first time—can make you feel both nervous and excited. If you are nervous, realize that you are in good company. Many biblical leaders, such as Moses, Joshua, and the apostle Paul, felt nervous and inadequate to lead others (see, for example, 1 Cor. 2:3). Yet God's grace was sufficient for them, just as it will be for you.

Some excitement is also natural. Your leadership is a gift to the others in the group. Keep in mind, however, that other group members also share responsibility for the group. Your role is simply to stimulate discussion by asking questions and encouraging people to respond. The suggestions listed below can help you to be an effective leader.

Preparing to Lead

1. Ask God to help you understand and apply the passage to your own life. Unless that happens, you will not be prepared to lead others.

2. Carefully work through each question in the study guide. Meditate and reflect on the passage as you formulate your answers.

3. Familiarize yourself with the leader's notes for the study. These will help you understand the purpose of the study and will provide valuable information about the questions in the study.

4. Pray for the various members of the group. Ask God to use these studies to make you better disciples of Jesus Christ.

5. Before the first meeting, make sure each person has a study guide. Encourage them to prepare beforehand for each study.

Leading the Study

1. Begin the study on time. If people realize that the study begins on schedule, they will work harder to arrive on time.

2. At the beginning of your first time together, explain that these studies are designed to be discussions, not lectures. Encourage

everyone to participate, but realize that some may be hesitant to speak during the first few sessions.

3. Read the introductory paragraph at the beginning of the discussion. This will orient the group to the passage being studied.

4. Read the passage aloud. You may choose to do this yourself, or you might ask for volunteers.

5. The questions in the guide are designed to be used just as they are written. If you wish, you may simply read each one aloud to the group. Or you may prefer to express them in your own words. Unnecessary rewording of the questions, however, is not recommended.

6. Don't be afraid of silence. People in the group may need time to think before responding.

7. Avoid answering your own questions. If necessary, rephrase a question until it is clearly understood. Even an eager group will quickly become passive and silent if they think the leader will do most of the talking.

8. Encourage more than one answer to each question. Ask, "What do the rest of you think?" or "Anyone else?" until several people have had a chance to respond.

9. Try to be affirming whenever possible. Let people know you appreciate their insights into the passage.

10. Never reject an answer. If it is clearly wrong, ask, "Which verse led you to that conclusion?" Or let the group handle the problem by asking them what they think about the question.

11. Avoid going off on tangents. If people wander off course, gently bring them back to the passage being considered.

12. Conclude your time together with conversational prayer. Ask God to help you apply those things that you learned in the study.

13. End on time. This will be easier if you control the pace of the discussion by not spending too much time on some questions or too little on others.

More suggestions and help are found in the book *Leading Bible Discussions* (InterVarsity Press). Reading it would be well worth your time.

Study One   *The Incomparable Christ*
Revelation 1:1–20

Purpose To elevate the worth and wonder of Christ to a place of supremacy in our hearts and minds, and to establish Christ's authority to finally conquer Satan and the power of death and hell.

Question 2 It would be helpful to cross-reference Psalms 1:1–3; 119:97–105; Proverbs 3:1–26; Luke 8:15; 2 Timothy 3:16–17. Draw attention to the threefold response to the Word of reading, hearing, and doing as a commitment for this study (James 1:21–27).

Question 3 The "seven spirits" is no doubt a reference to the sevenfold ministry of the Holy Spirit (see Isaiah 11:2) and perhaps the Spirit's ministry to the seven churches being addressed.

Question 6 For additional discussion see John 14:1–6; Acts 1:8–11, 1 Corinthians 15:50–58; and 1 John 3:1–3.

Question 9 For an in-depth description of these seven churches and their locations, see William Barclay, *The Revelation of St. John*, vol. 1, The Daily Study Bible: Ephesus, pp. 70ff.; Smyrna, pp. 89ff.; Pergamum, pp. 106ff.; Thyatira, pp. 125ff.; Sardis, pp. 142ff.; Philadelphia, pp. 158ff.; Laodicea, pp. 173ff.

Question 10 Too often we view Christ as pal, friend, Savior, creator, and advocate, but miss the reality of the awesome impact of his person as the Lord of Glory. Note John's response (v. 17). Like Isaiah (Isaiah 6:1–7) and John, if we were to see him we would not run up and hug him as our bosom buddy but would fall before him in awe and legitimate fear. Draw the group's attention to his tender and forgiving response to us in both Isaiah 6:7 and Revelation 1:17. Note as well that a clear view of the awesome majesty of Christ issues in a response of willing service to him (Isaiah 6:8; Revelation 1:19).

Question 11 It is important to point out that verses 17–18 set up the rest of the book as it ratifies Christ's authority to consummate ultimate conquest over Satan and his forces.

Study Two | *Great Expectations*
Revelation 2:1–11

Purpose   To develop the habit of focusing on seeing our lives in the light of Christ's expectations for us with a view toward pleasing him.

Question 2   Note that this section begins with a reference to the fact that Christ is present among us and manages angels that minister to us (cf. 1:20).

Question 3   Ephesus was the capital city of Asia Minor and was visited by Paul on his third missionary journey (Acts 19). Interestingly, it was John's home both before and after his exile to the Isle of Patmos (Revelation 1:9). The church at Ephesus was led by several key New Testament figures in addition to John: Aquila, Priscilla, Apollos, and Timothy.

Alan Johnson notes that the Christians at Ephesus "did not lack serious and sustained activity, even to the point of suffering for Christ's name" (*Expositor's Bible Commentary,* vol. 12, p. 433).

Question 5   The word *first* here refers not to time—that is, "when you first loved me"—but rather to priority, "doing all you do because you love me more than anything else."

Question 8   The concept of "overcomer" used throughout this section is not intended to mean that our salvation is dependent on our good works (cf. Ephesians 2:8–9). Charles C. Ryrie explains, "An overcomer is not someone who has some special power in the Christian life or someone who has learned some secret of victory. John himself defined an overcomer as a believer in Christ (1 John 5:4–5). Thus every Christian is an overcomer. . . . Believers here are promised the tree of life; that is, eternal life which was lost when Adam sinned in the garden (Gen. 2:9; 3:22; Rev. 22:2, 14)" (*Revelation,* Everyman's Bible Commentary, p. 23).

Living out the reality of our position as overcomers does not gain paradise for us but assures our hearts and minds that God will indeed keep his promises to us regarding eternity.

Question 10   In the early church, tribulation and poverty (the Greek word here, *ptocheia,* means the deepest kind of poverty) were often the result of social position (some members were slaves) or

72

their commitment to Christ (Christians often lost jobs, were ostracized by their families, or were the objects of ridicule in society).

Regarding riches in Christ, notice Psalm 73:22–28; John 14:2–3; 1 Corinthians 3:16; 2 Corinthians 8:9; Galatians 4:1–7; 1 John 3:1–3.

The reference to a synagogue of Satan means that although these Jews were religious, they were doing the work of Satan by inflicting suffering on the church.

Question 13 In regard to the promise at the end of verse 10, there were two kinds of crowns in the society that surrounded the New Testament church: crowns for royalty, and crowns given as rewards for victory. The image of victory crowns is used extensively in the New Testament, awarded for righteousness (2 Timothy 4:8), rejoicing (1 Thessalonians 2:19), glory (1 Peter 5:4). Here the reference is to the crown of life (see also James 1:12). These are crowns of victory, not nobility. They are rewards, not symbols of royalty.

Study Three

First Things First
Revelation 2:12–3:6

Purpose To understand how immorality, idolatry, and false teaching affect Christians and the life of the church, and to see Christ as the highest priority for our loyalty, purity, and fidelity to His Word.

Question 1 Malcolm Muggeridge once noted, "The most extraordinary thing about human beings [is the fact] that they pursue ends which they know to be disastrous and turn their backs on ways they know to be joyous" (quoted in Henry, *Twilight of a Great Civilization: The Drift Toward Neo-Paganism*, p. 21).

Henry underscores this when he observes, "Our generation is lost to the truth of God, to the reality of divine revelation, to the content of God's will, to the power of His redemption, and to the authority of His Word. For this loss it is paying dearly in a swift relapse to paganism. The savages are stirring again; you can hear them rumbling and rustling in the tempo of our times" (ibid., p. 15).

Question 2 "Where Satan has his throne" and "where Satan lives" are most likely references to the fact that Pergamum was the seat of the emperor worship that was required of all the citizens of the Roman Empire. There was also a large throne to the god Zeus on a nearby hillside. These cultural forces in that city defined clearly a Christian's commitment to have no other gods in their hearts but the true and living God. However, they had been compromised by the prevailing attitudes of their world and had fallen into the immoral practices that were celebrated in pagan idolatry.

Question 7   The "hidden manna" (v. 17) is a reference to God's sufficient supply for our lives in the face of need.

The "white stone" is most likely a reference to the legal practice of those times in which judges would give white stones to those who were acquitted of a charge and black stones to those who were condemned. The name on the stone might be the name "Jehovah"—which was never spoken aloud among the Old Testament Hebrews—or the name of the recipient. John Walvoord observes, "The giving of the white stone to the believer here, then, is the indication that he has been accepted or favored by Christ, a wonderful assurance especially for those who have been rejected by the wicked world and are the objects of its persecution" (*The Revelation of Jesus Christ: A Commentary,* p. 71).

Question 9   The mention of Jezebel is probably a reference to a woman who claimed the authority of a prophetess, yet who was not an authentic speaker of divine truth. She evidently urged Christians to continue their pagan worship of idols and the immorality that was associated with the idolatrous feasts.

This no doubt was not her actual name, but a name given to her to associate her evil influence with the wicked wife of King Ahab (see 1 Kings 21:1–16; 19:2).

Question 10   Ruling over the nations (vv. 26–27) refers to the faithful who will reign with Christ during his millennial kingdom.

The "morning star" (v. 28) refers to Christ (cf. Revelation 22:16) and is a wonderful picture of Christ representing an assurance of the glorious dawn of eternity.

Question 11   White robes (vv. 4–5) were symbols of festivity, victory, and purity. William Barclay wonders whether these are not a reference to the robes of our resurrection.

The "book of life" is most likely a reference to God's book in which the names of all human beings are recorded. Only those who have overcome through faith in Christ (cf. 1 John 5:4–5) will remain in the book. Again, this is an assurance that when we live as overcomers, we are confident that the overcoming work of grace is a reality for us (cf. Revelation 20:12).

In the world of early Christians, the whole population was recorded in a book of the king or ruler. At death, a person's name was deleted. Our assurance is that even death cannot expunge us from God's Book of Life.

Study Four
Opportunity Knocks
Revelation 3:7–22

Purpose   To focus on the privileges and opportunities we have in Christ and the issues in life that prevent us from going through the doors he opens for us.

Question 2   The holiness of Christ entails both his absolute purity and his complete uniqueness; it means that there is no one like him and that he is totally set apart (cf. Hosea 11:9).

The "key of David" may be a reference to Isaiah 22:20ff. Kings had keys that they alone held, which empowered them and symbolized their supreme authority. The key of David would refer to Christ's place in the line of David as the promised Messiah, and as such he holds all the authority and inherits all the promises made to David and his successive line of kings about the Messiah.

Question 4   You might take note of the pressures Peter was facing at the time of his denial of Christ (see John 13:36–38; 18:25–27).

Question 6   While there are differing opinions among evangelical scholars, this may be (and, to my mind, is) a reference to Christ's rapture of the church before the outpouring of God's wrath in the Great Tribulation as described in Revelation 6–19.

John Walvoord notes, "This passage therefore provides some support for the hope that Christ will come for His church before the time of trial and trouble described in Revelation 6 to 19. This time of tribulation will overtake the entire world, as God inflicts His wrath upon unbelieving Gentiles as well as upon Christ-rejecting

Jews" (*The Revelation of Jesus Christ: A Commentary,* p. 87).

Alan Johnson concludes, "In any event, we have here a marvelous promise of Christ's protection (*tēreō,* "keep") for those who have protected (*tēreō*) his word by their loving obedience" (*Expositor's Bible Commentary,* vol. 12, p. 455).

Question 9   Charles C. Ryrie notes, "Near Laodicea were hot mineral springs whose water could be drunk only if very hot. When lukewarm, it became nauseating" (*Revelation,* Everyman's Bible Commentary, p. 31). By contrast, cold water from a natural source is also pleasing and refreshing. "Hot" and "cold" are not to be understood as terms for spirituality, because Christ certainly would not commend spiritual coldness. Rather, he seems to be speaking here of a life that is intentional and well-motivated, and thus pleasing, not self-satisfied, complacent, or indifferent to real issues of discipleship.

Question 11   You might refer to Proverbs 3:11–12 and Hebrews 12:5–13.

Question 12   Given the context, this verse—though often applied to the lost, assuring them of God's desire to come into their lives—is better suited to Christ's desire for unhindered fellowship with those who have already put their faith in him.

Study Five
The Worthy-to-Be-Worshiped Christ
Revelation 4–5

Purpose   To recognize God and his Son, Jesus Christ, as the supreme rulers, worthy of unrestrained praise, and to give them due worship.

Question 2   It would be provocative to have the group specify the evil and injustice in our world that seem to go unchecked and unsettled. The knowledge that justice will be rendered perfectly and completely in a future age can give us confidence and courage to endure even the unfair trials of the present life.

Question 3   The Scriptures recount numerous ways in which humans have encountered the veiled splendor of God. The description here emphasizes again that ordinary persons cannot countenance

God in all his glory and majesty. He is beyond literal description.

Christ is introduced as "the Lamb" in chapter 5. The image of Christ as the Lamb is full of meaning. Merrill C. Tenney wrote, "The title *Lamb* stresses particularly His redemptive aspects since it is modified by the phrase 'as though it had been slain' (5:6, 9, 12; 13:8). Never is the exact word 'Lamb' used of Christ outside of Revelation, although a similar word meaning 'sacrificial lamb' occurs in four passages elsewhere (John 1:29, 36; Acts 8:32; 1 Peter 1:19)" (*Interpreting Revelation,* p. 174).

John Walvoord concludes, "the Lamb is represented as one sovereign in His own authority, omnipotent in power, and worthy as the Redeemer who died" (*The Revelation of Jesus Christ: A Commentary,* p. 115).

The identity of the elders seems best interpreted as individuals selected to be involved in Christ's governance. While some claim that these are angels, crowns are not associated with angels; nor does the designation *elder* seem fitting for angels. Crowns and white garments are promised to faithful *persons* in the immediate context of chapters 2 and 3. Christ promised thrones to the faithful who followed him (see Matthew 19:27–29).

William Barclay concludes, "The likeliest explanation of all is that the twenty-four elders are the symbolic representatives of the faithful people of God" (*The Revelation of John,* vol. 1, The Daily Study Bible, p. 194).

Question 4   Alan Johnson suggests that the lion stands for royal power; the ox, strength; the man, spirituality; and the eagle, swiftness of action. He adds that each of these is the pinnacle of its species (*Expositor's Bible Commentary,* vol. 12, p. 403).

Question 6   If you are in a group, you might consider setting apart an empty chair, representing the throne of God, and all kneeling before it and placing their lists of symbols upon it. Follow this with a period of silent meditation, or read aloud in unison the praise statement in verse 11. Then read responsively, from chapter 5, verses 11, 12, the first part of verse 13, and the second part of verse 13 with verse 14.

Sing together the chorus "Thou Art Worthy" or a song expressing a similar theme.

Question 7   The scroll contains the story of the completion of God's redemptive purposes and programs. Since it represents the unfolding of the consummation of God's victory over sin and his enthronement as the ultimate ruler through eternity, John is struck with sorrow that no one can open it and finish the work of redemption.

Question 9   You may want to refer to Colossians 1:13; Romans 12:1–2; 14:17; 1 Peter 2:9–12; Hebrews 13:15–16; Philippians 2:17.

Study Six   *The Lamb: The Merciful Judge*
Revelation 6:1–8:5

Purpose   To create a greater sense of appreciation for the necessity of judgment, the availability of mercy, and an awareness that both are fulfilled in Christ, who is the Lamb.

Question 1   Chapters 6 through 19 comprise the seven-year stretch of what is known as the Great Tribulation, when the judgments necessary to culminate Satan's dominion in human history are poured out on the earth. There are three sequences: the seven seals (ch. 6), seven trumpets (chs. 8–9), and seven bowls (ch. 16). They are not three different ways of looking at seven judgments; rather, they are sequential. These judgments conclude with the second coming of Christ (19:11–16). The material included between the judgments is additional information regarding this time of tribulation. It is my understanding of Scripture that the church is removed by the rapture before the judgments begin.

Question 3   The seals represent the Antichrist revealed (6:1–2), war (vv. 3–4), famine (vv. 5–6), death (vv. 7–8), martyrdom (vv. 9–11), and upheaval and terror (vv. 12–17).

There is a close resemblance here to Christ's prediction of the end times in his Olivet discourse (Matthew 24:5–9). There Christ calls these unfolding seals "the beginning of birth pains" (v. 8). Matthew 24 creates an instructive and fascinating backdrop to Revelation 6 to 19.

For a discussion of Christ as "the Lamb," see notes in study 5.

Question 4   Jim Elliot, a missionary who gave his life as a martyr in the jungles of Ecuador, wrote, "He is no fool who loses what he cannot keep to gain what he cannot lose."

When the German theologian Dietrich Bonhoeffer went to his death at the hands of the Nazis, his last words were, "Oh God, this is the end; but for me it is just the beginning."

You may want to refer to Romans 8:35–39; Philippians 1:21–23; Hebrews 11:35–12:4.

Question 6   A seal was used in New Testament times to guarantee ownership and security.

You may want to refer to 1 Corinthians 13; 2 Corinthians 4:7–11; Psalm 27.

Question 7   Note that the angels are so struck with God's mercy in the face of such sin and well-deserved judgment that they fall in awestruck worship before God. After an eternity of serving him they are still enamored with him, compelled to worship him and to affirm through their worship his justice expressed in judgment.

Question 8   Refer to the details of Psalm 23 in relation to Revelation 7:17 and its broader context (Revelation 6:1–8:4).

Question 9   The seventh seal is the next series of judgments (the seven trumpets) given to seven angels to execute.

Study Seven   *Trouble and Triumph*
Revelation 8:5–11:19

Purpose   To understand both the depravity of mankind and the powerful judgment of God, and to gain hope through the knowledge of God's ultimate triumph over evil and his righteous rule.

Question 1   This section of Revelation covers the judgments of the seven trumpets, which follow the judgments of the seals and occur just before the judgments of the bowls. All of these take place, in my view, during the last three and a half years of the Great Tribulation (cf. Daniel 9:27), in increasingly rapid succession.

The last three judgments of the trumpets are so devastating that they are called three "woes" (Revelation 8:13). Note throughout this section the intensity of the judgments, their means and focus (including the material world, the spirit world, the temple, and the two witnesses), the response of the population of the earth, and the culmination of Christ's reign.

Question 2   Throughout history men have worshiped the creation rather than the God of creation. God intended that his creation draw mankind's attention toward him. Instead, humans have elevated creation to the level of a god (as strikingly expressed in New Age thought) and seek to control the creation for their own consumption, pleasure, and glory.

In this section in particular, the point is made that Christ's role as creator and controller of creation is a primary credential for his rule and reign (Revelation 10:5–6).

Question 4   God intended that his creation would be preserved and cared for as part of mankind's stewardship of this visible evidence of God's glory. The current environmental movement seeks to preserve the created order with no thought of submission to or glory to God, but rather for mankind's safety and glory. Some of the more radical environmental movements are motivated by the notions that (a) the animal kingdom, the plant kingdom, and the rest of creation are of equal worth and value with humanity, and (2) the pantheistic premise that nature is God and that God is in all of nature.

Question 6   *Abyss* ("bottomless pit," KJV) in verses 1 and 11 is a Greek word that refers to the place where fallen angels are held in custody until the final judgment (Jude 6). These demons are angels who participated in Satan's prehistoric rebellion (see Isaiah 14:12; Luke 10:18). Their king, Satan, is called "destroyer" in both Hebrew and Greek.

See also 1 Peter 5:8 and Job 1.

Question 7   The four angels are four evil ones prepared by Satan for a massive slaughter of one third of the earth's population. They are restrained until this time by good angels, who release them to become instruments of God's judgment.

The golden altar in verse 13 may refer to the prayers of the saints of all time for their vindication and the judgment of evil (see Revelation 6:9 and 8:3).

The army of two hundred million (v. 16) is probably best thought of in terms of demons rather than men. Alan Johnson notes, "All the Allied and Axis forces at their peak in World War II were only about 70 million. . . . it seems better to understand the vast numbers and description of the horses as indicating demonic hordes. Such large numbers do occasionally indicate angelic hosts elsewhere in Scripture (Ps. 68:17; Rev. 5:11; cf. 2 Kings 2:11–12; 6:17). This would not eliminate the possibility of human armies of manageable size also being involved. But the emphasis here (vv. 16–19) is on their fully demonic character, utterly cruel and determined, showing no mercy to man, woman, or child. These demons might also be manifest in pestilences, epidemic diseases, or misfortunes as well as in armies. Such would explain the use of 'plagues' to describe these hordes (vv. 18, 20; cf. 11:6; 16:9, 21)" (*Expositor's Bible Commentary*, vol. 12, 494–95).

Question 8 The two purposes of these judgments were (a) to judge mankind for idolatry and corrupt lifestyle, and (b) to bring people to repentance (see Luke 13:3, 5; 2 Peter 3:9).

Note the correlation between the judgments of the first six trumpets and the list of sins in verses 20 and 21. The ten plagues in Egypt were focused on the gods that were worshiped in Egypt.

Question 10 It should be noted that Revelation 10:1–11:13 interrupts the flow of the seven trumpet judgments and inserts relevant information about John's experience. It is not intended that the account of the two witnesses fit within the time sequence of the seven trumpets.

Question 11 The measurement of the temple indicates God's observing and evaluating both the temple and its worshipers, and it may mean that the faithful worshipers are to be secured for blessing and kept from harm. This is a reference to the temple that will be in operation during the tribulation, where the man of sin will seat himself in the last days of the tribulation, demanding to be worshiped and overthrowing the worship of God.

The two witnesses are unidentified, though some think they are Moses and Elijah returned to the earth. Their ministry lasts exactly three and a half years. It is unclear whether they lead the ministry of the 144,000 in the first half of the tribulation and are defeated with the rise and empowerment of the anti-Christ, or they minister in the greater days of God's wrath in the second half of the tribulation.

Question 13 This last woe, the seventh trumpet, is a vision regarding the final conquest of Christ over all of creation, the judgment of sinners, and the reward of the faithful. It elicits the enthusiastic and spontaneous worship of saints and provides the confidence that this tragic and turbulent time that is being unfolded before John's eyes will indeed be resolved in righteousness, order, and complete victory.

Study Eight | *The Night Before Christmas*
Revelation 12

Purpose   To understand the invisible war being waged between God and Satan.

Question 3   Chapters 12–14 form another interlude, this time between the trumpet judgments and the bowls of God's wrath. As was true with the previous interludes (Revelation 7:1–17; 10:1–11:13), the information is not part of a time sequence but is important to a full understanding of what unfolds through the seven years of tribulation.

John Walvoord introduces this section with this summary: "In chapters 12 through 14 of the book of Revelation, the great actors of the tribulation time are introduced in another parenthetical section ending at 14:20. As many commentators have noted, they are seven in number: (1) the woman, representing Israel, (2) the dragon, representing Satan, (3) the man-child, referring to Christ, (4) Michael, representing the angels, (5) Israel, the remnant of the seed of the woman, (6) the beast out of the sea, the world dictator, and (7) the beast out of the earth, the false prophet and religious leader of the world. About these main characters swirls the tremendously moving scene of the great tribulation. First to be introduced and of prime importance as a key to the whole situation is the woman representing Israel" (*The Revelation of Jesus Christ: A Commentary,* p. 187).

Satan's vehement assault on Israel was focused on preventing the coming of the Messiah and only later was motivated by his anger toward the nation for her role in God's redemptive scheme. Many people feel—with good reason—that Hitler may have been demon possessed and that thereby accounts for his hatred and genocide of the Jews.

Question 4   Take note of the events surrounding Christ's birth; his temptation (Matthew 4); the hostility of religious leaders (Luke

4:29–30; John 10:22–39); the cross; and the Roman guards at the tomb (Matthew 28).

Question 5   See also Psalms 27:1–3; 118:5–9; Acts 1:9–11; Romans 8:35–39.

Question 6   See also Psalm 2:9; 1 Corinthians 15:24–28; Philippians 2:9–11; Revelation 11:15; 19:15.

Question 7   There is a massive time lapse between verses 5 and 6, which is not unusual in prophetic literature. Verse 6 concerns God's provision of safety and peace for Israel in the first three and a half years of the tribulation, as is noted by the time reference "1,260 days" (cf. Daniel 9:27).

Question 8   Scripture teaches that Satan has access to the presence of God (Job 1), where he accuses the faithful (Revelation 12:10) until he and his angels are barred from God's presence after a cosmic war with Michael and his angels. This victory takes place because of the victory of Christ on the cross and marks the beginning of the last three and a half years of the tribulation, when Satan's wrath against the earth and Israel will be poured out (vv. 12–13).

The fact that he had only a "short time" (v. 12) and that he poured out his wrath on believing Jews (v. 17) also indicates that Satan's expulsion from God's presence comes during the final stages of the tribulation. This expulsion brings great rejoicing with a hymn of victory (vv. 10–12). Christ's triumph over Satan assures faithful believers of victory even in the face of death and martyrdom (v. 11).

Question 9   See also Job 16:19; John 2:1–2.

Question 10   This angry outburst comprises Satan's final, massive—and unsuccessful—attempt to eliminate Israel as a race.

The phrase "a time, times and half a time" (v. 14) refers again to a three-and-a-half-year period, presumably the last half of the tribulation.

It is unclear what the imagery of the flood and the earth's swallowing it up actually means (v. 16).

Unable to annihilate the race, Satan turns finally to the faithful of Israel who have not fled to the wilderness (v. 17).

Marked for Good
Revelation 13–14

Purpose To establish for ourselves a clearer identity with Christ before the world in the face of great pressure from Satan.

Question 2 After Satan is cast to the earth, he creates and empowers a beast whose character is described in images of great authority and power. This beast is obviously positioned against God, since all its heads identify blasphemous names.

Although this beast is not called the great and final antichrist that is predicted in 1 John 2:18, 22, there is no doubt that this is he. Some, with good reason, see the beast as representing a confederation of nations led by a singular leader whose seat of authority is in Rome (see, for example, Charles C. Ryrie, *Revelation,* Everyman's Bible Commentary, p. 82). Alan Johnson finds in the beast's description "the hideous Satan-backed system of deception and idolatry that may at any time express itself in human systems of various kinds, such as Rome. Yet at the same time John also seems to be saying that this blasphemous, blaspheming, and blasphemy-producing reality will have a final, intense, and, for the saints, utterly devastating manifestation." Further, he says, "All three—the dragon, the sea beast, and the earth beast—though distinguishable, are nevertheless in collusion to effect the same end: the deception that led the world to worship the dragon and the sea beast and the destruction of all who oppose them" (*Expositor's Bible Commentary,* vol. 12, pp. 525–56).

The wound that was healed may be a reference to the victory won by Christ at the cross, which though finally fatal has not yet caused the demise of the power and influence of Satan.

Many have speculated regarding the identity of this beast (for example, a reincarnated Nero, Judas Iscariot, Hitler, or Stalin). In any case, it must be noted that he calls all the world to worship him and seeks to destroy all those who will not.

Question 3 This almost limitless power of Satan over both the world at large and the saints is exercised for the last three and a half years until the second coming of Christ terminates the reign of terror. Note the sovereignty of God in controlling the duration of Satan's reign.

Question 4 The reference in this passage to the book of life is problematic. The earlier book of life (Revelation 3:5) held all the names of mankind in the manner of the books that kings kept, whereas this reference indicates that only those who are truly saved are in this, the Lamb's book of life (cf. Revelation 17:8; 20:12, 15; 21:27). It is best to understand that God in his divine foreknowledge wrote the names of all the saints of all time in this, *his* Lamb's book of life.

Question 5 Verse 10 refers to God's certain vindication of persecuted saints, which forms a basis for steadfastness and faith even unto death. See also Romans 12:17–21; 1 Corinthians 15:55–58; 1 Peter 2:19–25.

Question 6 Note that Satan throughout history has used deceit to gain a following (see Genesis 3:1–6; John 8:44). His power to support his deceit with supernatural activity is noted in Exodus 7:11–12 and has been witnessed in occult activity by missionaries and others who have been exposed to environments where spiritism prevails.

Question 7 This is no doubt a vision of the ultimate triumph of the redeemed with Christ in heaven. Note that in the deepest moment of trouble and intimidation, God inserts the assurance of ultimate final deliverance and victory.

You may wish to read or sing a hymn in place of silent meditation. An old Swedish hymn, "More Secure Is No One Ever," speaks of our safety and security in Christ. The pilgrim song "Victory in Jesus" underscores our confidence in Christ.

Question 9 Babylon the Great is a metaphorical reference to the evil and corrupting system and authority of the dragon, his beast and false prophet, that has been spectacularly and ruthlessly imposed on the earth.

Leon Morris notes, "In every case Babylon is called 'great.' There is no reason for holding that John means the Mesopotamian city of this name (though he may well have in mind Je. li.7f.). In the first mention of this city in the Bible (Gn. xi.9, but cf. Gn. x.10) we read that after the Flood man tried to scale the heights of heaven by building a mighty tower. The name thus stands for the pride of man and for the heathen city-empire. . . . John is looking forward to the overthrow of all the evil that Babylon stands for" (*The Revelation of St. John: An Introduction and Commentary*, p. 180).

Study Ten

I Don't Get Mad . . .
Revelation 15–16

Purpose To understand God's wrath as an expression of his holiness, and to respond with praise for his mercy and grace to those who know him.

Question 2 God's wrath reaches a point when it is finished (v. 1). It is righteous, true, and grounded in his rightful authority (v. 3). Our anger may be ongoing, sinful, and inappropriate in that we exact vengeance outside the bounds of our authority.

Question 3 The world has little tolerance for a God who expresses wrath and judgment. Christ's followers must understand not only the necessity of God's judgment, but also its relationship to his holiness and righteousness and its being exercised in ways that are right and true (see Revelation 19:11).

Note that throughout the book of Revelation God's judgments are preceded by and interrupted by the praise and affirmation of the angels and the faithful (see Revelation 5:12–14; 7:9–12; 11:15–17; 12:10–12; 14:1–3, 7; 15:3–4; 16:5–7; 17:14; 19:1–6).

Question 4 The "fear" of God is not fright or intimidation. Rather, it is an awestruck response to his supreme presence that produces spontaneous submission. To glorify God means to seek to use all that we are and have to reflect him and enhance his reputation.

Even when God's mighty works (in this context, works of judgment) are intimately and intensely felt, the sinful world sets their hearts against him rather than repentantly fearing and glorifying his name.

(Note that the references to Christ the Lamb as King [vv. 3–4] refer to the coming millennial reign of Christ.)

Question 5 This picture forces us to see God's judgment, not as arbitrary and vindictive but rather as a rightful outgrowth of his holiness, demonstrating that he is indeed holy and righteous.

John Walvoord notes that "the Testimony" (v. 5) is a reference to the tablets of the Ten Commandments kept in the Holy of Holies in the tabernacle. These served as a reminder that judgment is based on the righteous standards that have been so ruthlessly violated throughout history. Of this powerful picture, Walvoord writes, "The Holy of Holies in the heavenly Tabernacle is opened. The expression 'the temple' (Gr., *naos*) refers to the inner holy place of the Tabernacle.... The whole scene is most symbolic of what is about to happen. The angels coming out of the sanctuary indicate that the judgments to be poured out stem from the holiness of God and are properly required of God who must do all things right.... If gold reflects the glory of God, it would point to the conclusion that these angels pouring out righteous judgments on the earth thereby bring glory to God" (*The Revelation of Jesus Christ: A Commentary*, p. 229).

Question 6   When Christians refuse the mark of the beast it is in an environment that threatens everything in their lives even to the point of death. It seems that evil is the permanent, dominant force and that all the world is cooperating and enjoying an alliance with the antichrist. See also Galatians 6:7–8.

Question 7   See Psalm 37:1–11.

Question 8   See Proverbs 3:7–12 and Hebrews 12:5–11.

Question 9   We can cite several instances in Scripture when God's judgment fulfilled practical ends in the world in addition to expressing his holiness. Consider the judgments on Sodom and Gomorrah (Deuteronomy 29:23; Isaiah 1:9), the drowning of the Egyptians in the Red Sea (Exodus 14:21–31), the defeat of pagan cultures by Israel (Joshua 2:3–11), and Jonah's proclamation of judgment on Nineveh (Jonah 3; Matthew 12:41).

God's purpose in drying up the Euphrates River is to enable the rulers of the world to join the battle of Armageddon (v. 16; see Daniel 11:44), where the final war of mankind against God will be staged. This is a dramatic note regarding the sovereignty of God, who is guiding and managing even the strategies of those armies massed in opposition to him, even though they are demon filled (v. 14).

Question 10   This verse does not refer to the rapture of the church, but instead to Jesus' second coming to defeat personally the forces of evil. Yet the same sense of imminence is attached to this event.

Note the practical impact on our lives that Scripture indicates follows an anticipation of that day (John 14:1–6; 1 Corinthians 15:50–58; 1 Thessalonians 5:1–11; 1 John 3:1–3).

Study Eleven   *Clearing the Way*
Revelation 17–18

Purpose   To become aware of how Satan works in the world, and to see how God's sovereignty is revealed in the final judgment and conquest of sin.

Question 1   See John 8:42–44, 12:31; James 1:13–16; 1 John 2:15–17 in regard to the conspiracy of Satan.

Concerning this passage, "Babylon" is a difficult concept to interpret specifically, but underlying all the views of Revelation there is agreement that it represents the systems of evil managed and maintained by Satan in this world. In particular it refers to the system of false religion (a one-world church, ch. 17) and the corrupt political systems that foster evil societies and cultures (ch. 18).

William Barclay describes in detail the religious and political debauchery in Rome, the Babylon of Christ's day (*The Revelation of John,* vol. 2, The Daily Study Bible). The apostle John, in writing the book of Revelation, would have understood the symbol of Babylon as representing such depravity.

Alan Johnson notes, "Babylon is an eschatological symbol of satanic deception and power.... It may be said that Babylon represents the total culture of the world apart from God, while the divine system is depicted by the New Jerusalem" (*Expositor's Bible Commentary,* vol. 12, p. 554). John Walvoord concludes, "The subject of Babylon in the Scripture is one of the prominent themes of the Bible beginning in Genesis 10, where the city of Babel is first mentioned, with continued references throughout the Scriptures climaxing here in the book of Revelation. From these various passages, it becomes clear that Babylon in Scripture is the name for a great system of religious error" (Walvoord, *The Revelation of Jesus Christ: A Commentary,* p. 246).

Question 4   An example is the Pharisees, who, though orthodox to the particulars, were spiritually adulterous in that they gave their ritualistic applications of the law equal weight with God's law and became proud, using their religion to enhance their status and power.

Question 5   See 1 Peter 5:8.

Question 6   Some examples: God used Satan's attacks on Job to demonstrate to a watching heavenly host that he was worthy to be worshiped and praised regardless of whether he blessed mankind or not (Job 1); the burden of extra work in Egypt strengthened the Israelites for their journey in the wilderness; the death of Christ to accomplish redemption (see Romans 8:29).

Question 7   See Jeremiah 9:23; Psalm 20:7; 147:10–11; 1 Timothy 6:17–19.

Study Twelve   *How Sweet It Will Be . . .*
      Revelation 19–22

Purpose   To develop a sense of confidence and anticipation regarding the final victory of Christ and our eternal delight with him in heaven.

Question 1   See John 14:1–6; 1 Corinthians 15:50–58; 1 John 3:1–3.

Question 2   Peggy Noonan, former speech writer for Presidents Reagan and Bush, writes, "I think we have lost the old knowledge that happiness is overrated—that, in a way, life is overrated. We have lost, somehow, a sense of mystery—about us, our purpose, our meaning, our role. Our ancestors believed in two worlds, and understood this to be the solitary, poor, nasty, brutish and short one. We are the first generations of man that actually expected to find happiness here on earth, and our search for it has caused such—unhappiness. The reason: If you do not believe in another, higher world, if you believe only in the flat material world around you, if you believe that this is your only chance at happiness—if that is what you believe, then you are not disappointed when the world does not give you a good measure of its riches, you are despairing." ("You'd Cry Too," *Forbes*, 14 September 1992, p. 65).

C. S. Lewis in *Mere Christianity* notes: "Hope is one of the Theological virtues. This means that a continual looking forward to the eternal world is not (as some modern people think) a form of

meant to do. It does not mean that we are to leave the present world as it is. If you read history you will find that the Christians who did most for the present world were just those who thought most of the next. The Apostles themselves, who set on foot the conversion of the Roman Empire, the great men who built up the Middle Ages, the English Evangelicals who abolished the Slave Trade, all left their mark on Earth, precisely because their minds were occupied with Heaven. It is since Christians have largely ceased to think of the other world that they have become so ineffective in this. Aim at heaven and you'll get earth thrown in; aim at earth and you'll get neither."

Question 4 Of the metaphor of our marriage to Christ, William Barclay writes, "In any marriage there must be four things, if the marriage is to be real, and these four things must also be in the relationship between the Christian and Christ. (i) There is *love*. The whole relationship is based on love, for a loveless marriage is a contradiction in terms. (ii) There is *intimate communion*. So intimate is the communion of man and wife that they become one flesh. The relationship of the Christian and Christ must be the closest relationship in all life. (iii) There is *joy*. There is nothing like the joy of loving and of being loved. If Christianity does not bring joy, it does not bring anything. (iv) There is *fidelity*. No marriage is real and no marriage can last without fidelity, and the Christian must be as faithful to Jesus Christ as Jesus Christ is to him" (*The Revelation of John*, vol. 2, *The Daily Study Bible*, p. 223).

All these characteristics (and more) will be ours with him in fullest measure in eternity.

Alan Johnson notes, "The wedding is the beginning of the earthly kingdom of God, the bride is the church in all her purity, the invited guests are both the bride and people who have committed themselves to Jesus" (*Expositor's Bible Commentary*, vol. 12, p. 572).

Question 6 Christ comes as a warrior to defeat Satan and the armies of this world at the battle of Armageddon.

Question 7 This is most likely a reference to the authority Jesus carries as Savior through his shed blood (perhaps a reference to the blood of the martyrs as well) and the authority of the edict of the Almighty God of the Universe.

Question 8   The thousand-year reign of Christ fulfills the kingdom promises to Israel. His reign is shared with faithful saints from the church, resurrected martyrs from the tribulation, and faithful Jews who lived through the tribulation and into the Millennium. Satan is bound, and Christ rules in righteousness and peace.

Question 12   In addition to the marvelous descriptions of heaven that John gives in this passage, Paul writes that "dying is gain" and "to depart and be with Christ" is far better (Philippians 1:21–23). This is perhaps the most profound description of heaven. It is far better than anything we can experience on earth. The center point will be a completed relationship with Christ.

BIBLIOGRAPHY

Barclay, William. *The Revelation of John*. The Daily Study Bible. 2 Volumes. Philadelphia: Westminster Press, 1959.

Henry, Carl F. H. *Twilight of a Great Civilization: The Drift Toward Neo-Paganism*. Westchester, Ill.: Crossway, 1988.

Johnson, Alan F. "Revelation." *The Expositor's Bible Commentary*. Volume 12. Ed. Frank E. Gaebelein. Grand Rapids: Zondervan, 1981.

Lewis, C. S. *Mere Christianity*. New York: Macmillan, 1978.

Morris, Leon. *The Revelation of St. John: An Introduction and Commentary*. Grand Rapids: Wm. B. Eerdmans, 1969.

Noonan, Peggy. "You'd Cry Too." *Forbes*, 14 September 1992.

Ryrie, Charles C. *Revelation*. Everyman's Bible Commentary. Chicago: Moody Press, 1968.

Walvoord, John F. *The Revelation of Jesus Christ: A Commentary*. Chicago: Moody Press, 1966.